Easy Home Cooking™

Country Casseroles

PUBLICATIONS INTERNATIONAL, LTD.

Easy Home Cooking™

Country Casseroles

p. 14

p. 64

p. 80

The Basics

Whether you're making an everyday meal or planning for company, casseroles are perfect for any occasion. These warm, satisfying meals take you back to comforting memories of home-style cooking and are sure to have your family asking for more. Take advantage of the convenience of cooking casseroles and enjoy warm, home-cooked meals, especially when you don't have a lot of time to cook.

CASSEROLE COOKWARE

Casserole cookware comes in a variety of shapes, sizes and materials that fall into 2 general descriptions. They can be either deep, round containers with handles and tight-fitting lids or square and rectangular baking dishes. Casseroles are made out of glass, ceramic or metal. When making a casserole, it's important to bake the casserole in the proper size dish so that the ingredients cook evenly in the time specified. If you don't have the size or shape casserole listed in the recipe, another dish can often be substituted. Check the chart on page 7 for possible substitutions.

Size Unknown?

If the size of the casserole or baking dish isn't marked on the bottom of the dish, it can be measured to determine the size.

Round and oval casseroles are measured by volume, not inches, and are always listed by quart capacity. Fill a measuring cup with water and pour it into an empty casserole. Repeat until the casserole is filled with water, keeping track of the amount of water added. The amount of water is equivalent to the size of the dish.

Square and rectangular baking dishes are usually measured in inches. If the dimensions aren't marked on the bottom of a square or rectangular baking dish, use a ruler to measure on top from the inside of one edge to the inside of the edge across.

HELPFUL PREPARATION TECHNIQUES

Some of the recipes call for advance preparations, such as cooked chicken or pasta. In order to ensure success when following and preparing the recipes, here are several preparation tips and techniques.

Tips for Cooking Meat and Poultry

Two cooking methods commonly used when assembling casseroles are sautéing and poaching.

Sautéing is a quick-cooking method that can be used to cook meat and poultry. It promotes even cooking and produces a crisp, brown surface that locks in flavorful juices. The meat or poultry should be cut into even-size pieces, such as cubes or strips, so that they cook in the same amount of time.

Heat a small amount of cooking oil or other fat in a skillet over medium-high heat until hot. The meat or poultry is added and quickly turned or tossed in the oil or fat. The heat is then reduced and the meat or poultry is gently cooked to completion.

SUBSTITUTION GUIDE

Casserole Capacity	Baking Dish Size	Cups
1 quart	8-inch pie plate	4
1½ quarts	8×8×1½-inch 11×7-inch	6
2 quarts	8×8×2-inch 9×9×1½-inch 9-inch deep-dish pie plate	8
2½ quarts	9×9×2-inch	10
3½ to 4 quarts	13×9-inch	14 to 16

Make sure the skillet is large enough so that the food is not overcrowded.

To test for doneness, cut a few pieces to make sure they are no longer pink in centers.

Poaching is a cooking method suitable for preparing chicken. Fill a saucepan or stockpot with enough liquid, such as cold water or broth, to completely cover the chicken. Bring the water to a gentle simmer and add the chicken. Maintain an even, gentle simmer and make sure the chicken is fully submerged. Do not allow the water to boil. Remove the chicken when it is completely cooked and no longer pink in the center.

Meat from poached chicken is mild in flavor and tender and juicy in texture. Poached chicken is generally used for casseroles, salads and sandwiches.

To dice cooked chicken, place chicken on cutting board. Slice chicken lengthwise into strips; cut crosswise into pieces.

To shred cooked chicken, place chicken on cutting board. Pull chicken into long shreds with two forks.

Tips for Cooking Pasta

Here are some basics to remember when cooking pasta. For every pound of pasta, bring 4 to 6 quarts of water to a full, rolling boil. Gradually add pasta,

allowing water to return to a boil. Stir frequently to prevent the pasta from sticking together.

Pasta is finished cooking when it is tender but still firm to the bite, or al dente. The pasta continues to cook when the casserole is placed in the oven so it is important that the pasta be slightly undercooked. Otherwise, the more the pasta cooks, the softer it becomes and, eventually, it will fall apart.

Immediately drain pasta to prevent overcooking. For best results, combine pasta with other ingredients immediately after draining.

Tips for Cooking Rice

The different types of rice require different amounts of water and cooking times. Follow the package instructions for the best results. Here are some general tips to keep in mind when cooking rice.

Measure the amount of water specified on the package and pour into a medium saucepan. Bring to a boil over medium-high heat. Slowly add rice and return to a boil. Reduce heat to low. Cover and simmer for the time specified on the package or until the rice is tender and most of the water has been absorbed.

To test the rice for doneness, bite into a grain or squeeze a grain between your thumb and

index finger. The rice is done when it is tender and the center is not hard.

Tips for Chopping and Storing Fresh Herbs

To chop fresh herbs, place in glass measuring cup. Snip herbs into small pieces with kitchen scissors.

Wrap remaining fresh herbs in a slightly damp paper towel and place in an airtight plastic food storage bag. Store up to 5 days in the refrigerator.

TOP IT OFF!

Buttery, golden brown bread crumbs are a popular choice when it comes to topping a casserole but the selections shouldn't end there. Be creative with the many choices available to jazz up an old favorite or just vary how they are used. Crispy toppings can be crushed, partially crushed, broken into

bite-size pieces or left whole. Fruits, vegetables and other toppings can be chopped, sliced or shredded. Sprinkle a new spice or herb in place of another one. All the toppings can be placed on top of the casserole in a variety of ways—a small amount in the center, around the edges as a border or in straight or diagonal lines across the top.

Crispy toppings add a nice texture to your casseroles. Choose from crushed unsweetened cereals; potato, corn, tortilla or bagel chips; pretzels; flour or corn tortilla strips; plain or flavored croutons; flavored crackers; crumbled bacon; ramen or chow mein noodles; sesame seeds; French fried onions and various nuts. As a guide, add 1 tablespoon melted margarine to ½ cup crushed crumbs. Sprinkle over casserole and bake to add buttery flavor.

Fruits, vegetables and other toppings add a burst of color to most casseroles. Add green, red or white onions; orange or lemon peel; mushrooms; dried or fresh fruits, such as apples, apricots, cranberries, dates, oranges, pineapple and raisins; olives; bell or chili peppers; bean sprouts; tomatoes; avocados; celery; corn; coconut; carrots; fresh herbs and shredded cheeses according to

what flavor and look you desire. In order to keep the fruits and vegetables bright and crisp, add them 5 minutes before the casserole is finished cooking or sprinkle them on after it's out of the oven.

Homemade Bread Crumbs

Making your own bread crumbs is a great way to use up the rest of a fresh loaf. To make bread crumbs, preheat oven to 300°F. Place a single layer of bread slices on a baking sheet and bake 5 to 8 minutes or until completely dry and lightly browned. Cool completely. Process in food processor or crumble in resealable plastic food storage bag until very fine. For additional flavor, season with salt, pepper and a small amount of dried herbs, ground spices or grated cheese as desired. Generally, 1 slice of bread equals ⅓ cup bread crumbs.

Toasted Nuts

Toasting nuts intensifies their flavor and gives a boost to any casserole. To toast nuts, preheat oven to 350°F. Place a single layer of nuts on a baking sheet and bake until golden brown, stirring occasionally. Bake almonds, pecans and walnuts 5 to 10 minutes; hazelnuts 8 to 10 minutes and pine nuts 3 to 6 minutes. Sprinkle the nuts over the casserole after it is baked.

Because nuts have a high fat content, they become rancid quickly. Purchase small amounts at a time and use as soon as possible.

FREEZING CONVENIENCE

Most casseroles freeze very well and are popular for that reason. With today's hectic lifestyles, the convenience of casseroles is very appealing. Prepare the casserole when you have time and then freeze it. Then all you need to do is defrost and cook the casserole in order to serve a well-balanced dish with relative ease at your convenience.

To Freeze:

1. Line casserole or baking dish with plastic wrap, folding plastic wrap over edge of casserole. Spray with nonstick cooking spray.

2. Add combined casserole ingredients to lined casserole and place in freezer.

3. When frozen, lift food from casserole by lifting plastic wrap by the edges. Wrap airtight in freezer paper or place in resealable plastic freezer food storage bags, removing as much air as possible to prevent freezer burn.

4. Return casserole to freezer.

To Cook:

1. Remove casserole from freezer and discard all freezer and plastic wrap.

2. Place in original container; cover and place in the refrigerator to defrost.*

3. Bake in preheated oven according to recipe.

*Some casseroles can be placed directly in the oven without defrosting. Generally, the cooking time needs to be doubled, but begin checking for doneness 15 minutes before the final time.

Freezing Tips

- Casseroles made with condensed soup freeze well.

- Cook pasta and rice just until tender, but still chewy, to avoid overcooking during reheating.

- Cooked pasta and rice freeze well in resealable plastic food storage bags. These are convenient to have on hand when preparing casseroles.

- Freeze the casserole in individual serving size containers for a quick meal anytime.

- Double the recipe and freeze the second casserole for another meal.

Breakfast & Brunch

Egg & Sausage Casserole

½ pound pork sausage
3 tablespoons margarine or butter, divided
2 tablespoons all-purpose flour
¼ teaspoon salt
¼ teaspoon black pepper
1¼ cups milk

2 cups frozen hash brown potatoes
4 eggs, hard boiled and thinly sliced
½ cup cornflake crumbs
¼ cup sliced green onions
Fresh dill and oregano sprigs and chives (optional)

PREHEAT oven to 350°F. Spray 2-quart oval casserole with nonstick cooking spray. Crumble sausage into large skillet; brown over medium-high heat until no longer pink, stirring to separate sausage. Drain sausage on paper towels. Discard fat and wipe skillet with paper towel.

MELT 2 tablespoons margarine in same skillet over medium heat. Stir in flour, salt and pepper until smooth. Gradually stir in milk; cook and stir until thickened. Add sausage, potatoes and eggs; stir to combine. Pour into prepared dish. Melt remaining 1 tablespoon margarine. Combine cornflake crumbs and melted margarine in small bowl; sprinkle evenly over sausage mixture.

BAKE, uncovered, 30 minutes or until hot and bubbly. Sprinkle with onions. Garnish, if desired. *Makes 6 servings*

Nutrients per Serving: Calories: 371, Total Fat: 23 g, Protein: 14 g, Carbohydrate: 27 g, Cholesterol: 167 mg, Sodium: 600 mg, Dietary Fiber: 1 g Dietary Exchanges: Bread: 2, Meat: 1, Fat: 4

Mexican Roll-Ups with Avocado Sauce

8 eggs
2 tablespoons milk
1 tablespoon margarine or
   butter
1½ cups (6 ounces) shredded
   Monterey Jack cheese
1 large tomato, seeded and
   chopped
¼ cup chopped fresh
   cilantro
8 (6-inch) corn or flour
   tortillas

1½ cups salsa
2 medium avocados,
   chopped
¼ cup reduced-calorie sour
   cream
2 tablespoons diced green
   chilies
1 tablespoon fresh lemon
   juice
1 teaspoon hot pepper
   sauce
¼ teaspoon salt

PREHEAT oven to 350°F. Spray 13×9-inch baking dish with nonstick cooking spray.

WHISK eggs and milk in medium bowl until blended. Melt margarine in large skillet over medium heat; add egg mixture to skillet. Cook and stir 5 minutes or until eggs are set, but still soft. Remove from heat. Stir in cheese, tomato and cilantro.

SPOON about ⅓ cup egg mixture evenly down center of each tortilla. Roll up tortillas and place seam side down in prepared dish. Pour salsa evenly over tortillas. Cover tightly with foil and bake 20 minutes or until heated through.

Meanwhile, **PROCESS** avocados, sour cream, chilies, lemon juice, hot pepper sauce and salt in food processor or blender until smooth. Serve roll-ups with avocado sauce.   *Makes 8 servings*

Nutrients per Serving: Calories: 316, Total Fat: 22 g, Protein: 15 g, Carbohydrate: 16 g, Cholesterol: 234 mg, Sodium: 665 mg, Dietary Fiber: 7 g Dietary Exchanges: Bread: 1, Meat: 1½, Fat: 3½

Cook's Nook

To reduce fat, omit avocado sauce and serve with additional salsa and nonfat sour cream.

Breakfast Pizza

1 can (10 ounces)
  refrigerated biscuit
  dough
½ pound bacon slices
2 tablespoons margarine or
  butter
2 tablespoons all-purpose
  flour

¼ teaspoon salt
⅛ teaspoon black pepper
1½ cups milk
½ cup (2 ounces) shredded
  sharp Cheddar cheese
¼ cup sliced green onions
¼ cup chopped red bell
  pepper

PREHEAT oven to 350°F. Spray 13×9-inch baking dish with nonstick cooking spray.

SEPARATE biscuit dough and arrange side by side in rectangle on lightly floured surface without overlapping. Roll into 14×10-inch rectangle. Place in prepared dish; pat edges up sides of dish. Bake 15 minutes. Remove from oven and set aside.

Meanwhile, **PLACE** bacon in single layer in large skillet; cook over medium heat until crisp. Remove from skillet; drain on paper towels. Crumble and set aside.

MELT margarine in medium saucepan over medium heat. Stir in flour, salt and black pepper until smooth. Gradually stir in milk; cook and stir until thickened. Stir in cheese until melted. Spread sauce evenly over baked crust. Sprinkle bacon, green onions and bell pepper over sauce.

BAKE, uncovered, 20 minutes or until crust is golden brown.

Makes 6 servings

Nutrients per Serving: Calories: 280, Total Fat: 14 g, Protein: 10 g,
Carbohydrate: 29 g, Cholesterol: 18 mg, Sodium: 793 mg, Dietary Fiber: 1 g
Dietary Exchanges: Bread: 2, Meat: ½, Fat: 2½

Chili Cheese Puff

¾ cup all-purpose flour
1½ teaspoons baking powder
9 eggs
4 cups (16 ounces)
    shredded Monterey
    Jack cheese
2 cups (1 pint) 1% milkfat
    cottage cheese

2 cans (4 ounces each)
    diced green chilies,
    drained
1½ teaspoons sugar
¼ teaspoon salt
⅛ teaspoon hot pepper
    sauce
1 cup salsa

PREHEAT oven to 350°F. Spray 13×9-inch baking dish with nonstick cooking spray.

COMBINE flour and baking powder in small bowl.

WHISK eggs in large bowl until blended; add Monterey Jack cheese, cottage cheese, chilies, sugar, salt and hot pepper sauce. Add flour mixture; stir just until combined. Pour into prepared dish.

BAKE, uncovered, 45 minutes or until egg mixture is set. Let stand 5 minutes before serving. Serve with salsa. *Makes 8 servings*

Nutrients per Serving: Calories: 393, Total Fat: 23 g, Protein: 29 g, Carbohydrate: 14 g, Cholesterol: 292 mg, Sodium: 1060 mg, Dietary Fiber: 2 g Dietary Exchanges: Bread: 1, Meat: 4, Fat: 2

Cook's Nook

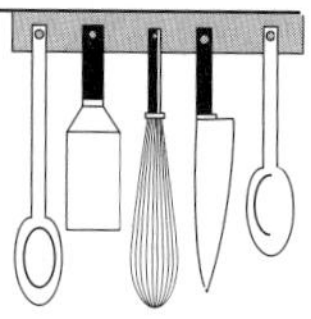

Substitute a jalapeño pepper for the diced green chilies. Seed and dice the jalapeño and add to egg mixture. Be careful when handling pepper because it can sting and irritate the skin. Wash hands after handling.

Menu

Chili Cheese Puff

Sausage Patties

Mango or Papaya Slices

Assorted Muffins

Orange Juice

Apple & Raisin Oven Pancake

1 large baking apple, cored
    and thinly sliced
⅓ cup golden raisins
2 tablespoons packed
    brown sugar
½ teaspoon ground
    cinnamon
4 eggs

⅔ cup milk
⅔ cup all-purpose flour
2 tablespoons margarine or
    butter, melted
Powdered sugar
    (optional)
Raspberries and fresh
    herb (optional)

PREHEAT oven to 350°F. Spray 9-inch pie plate with nonstick cooking spray.

COMBINE apple, raisins, brown sugar and cinnamon in medium bowl. Transfer to prepared pie plate.

BAKE, uncovered, 10 to 15 minutes or until apple begins to soften. Remove from oven. *Increase oven temperature to 450°F.*

Meanwhile, **WHISK** eggs, milk, flour and margarine in medium bowl until blended. Pour batter over apple mixture.

BAKE 15 minutes or until pancake is golden brown. Sprinkle with powdered sugar, if desired. Garnish with raspberries and herb, if desired.

Makes 6 servings

Nutrients per Serving: Calories: 207, Total Fat: 8 g, Protein: 7 g, Carbohydrate: 28 g, Cholesterol: 144 mg, Sodium: 103 mg, Dietary Fiber: 1 g
Dietary Exchanges: Fruit: 1, Bread: 1, Meat: ½, Fat: ½

Cook's Nook

Apple varieties best for baking are Cortland, Northern Spy, Rome Beauty, Winesap and York Imperial.

French Toast Strata

4 ounces day-old French or
Italian bread, cut into
¾-inch cubes (4 cups)
⅓ cup golden raisins
1 package (3 ounces)
cream cheese, cut into
¼-inch cubes
3 eggs
1½ cups milk

½ cup maple-flavored
pancake syrup
1 teaspoon vanilla
2 tablespoons sugar
1 teaspoon ground
cinnamon
Additional maple-flavored
pancake syrup
(optional)

SPRAY 11×7-inch baking dish with nonstick cooking spray. Place
bread cubes in even layer in prepared dish; sprinkle raisins and
cream cheese evenly over bread.

BEAT eggs in medium bowl with electric mixer at medium speed until
blended. Add milk, ½ cup pancake syrup and vanilla; mix well. Pour
egg mixture evenly over bread mixture. Cover; refrigerate at least
4 hours or overnight.

PREHEAT oven to 350°F. Combine sugar and cinnamon in small
bowl; sprinkle evenly over bread mixture.

BAKE, uncovered, 40 to 45 minutes or until puffy, golden brown and
knife inserted in center comes out clean. Cut into squares and serve
with additional pancake syrup, if desired.   *Makes 6 servings*

*Nutrients per Serving: Calories: 287, Total Fat: 9 g, Protein: 8 g, Carbohydrate: 44 g,
Cholesterol: 127 mg, Sodium: 237 mg, Dietary Fiber: trace
Dietary Exchanges: Fruit: 1, Bread: 2, Meat: ½, Fat: 1*

Beef & Pork

Chili Spaghetti Casserole

8 ounces uncooked
    spaghetti
1 pound lean ground beef
1 medium onion, chopped
¼ teaspoon salt
⅛ teaspoon black pepper
1 can (15 ounces)
    vegetarian chili with
    beans
1 can (14½ ounces) Italian-
    style stewed tomatoes,
    undrained

1½ cups (6 ounces) shredded
    sharp Cheddar cheese,
    divided
½ cup reduced-fat sour
    cream
1½ teaspoons chili powder
¼ teaspoon garlic powder

PREHEAT oven to 350°F. Spray 13×9-inch baking dish with nonstick cooking spray.

COOK pasta according to package directions until al dente. Drain and place in prepared dish.

Meanwhile, **PLACE** beef and onion in large skillet; sprinkle with salt and pepper. Brown beef over medium-high heat until beef is no longer pink, stirring to separate beef. Drain fat. Stir in chili, tomatoes with juice, 1 cup cheese, sour cream, chili powder and garlic powder.

ADD chili mixture to pasta; stir until pasta is well coated. Sprinkle with remaining ½ cup cheese.

COVER tightly with foil and bake 30 minutes or until hot and bubbly. Let stand 5 minutes before serving. *Makes 8 servings*

Nutrients per Serving: Calories: 347, Total Fat: 13 g, Protein: 23 g, Carbohydrate: 32 g, Cholesterol: 51 mg, Sodium: 414 mg, Dietary Fiber: 4 g
Dietary Exchanges: Vegetable: 1, Bread: 1½, Meat: 2½, Fat: 1½

Ham, Barley and Almond Bake

½ cup slivered almonds
1 tablespoon margarine or
    butter
1 cup uncooked barley
1 cup chopped carrots
1 bunch green onions,
    sliced
2 ribs celery, sliced
3 cloves garlic, minced
1 pound lean smoked ham,
    cubed
2 teaspoons dried basil
    leaves

1 teaspoon dried oregano
    leaves
¼ teaspoon black pepper
2 cans (14 ounces each)
    reduced-sodium beef
    broth
½ pound fresh green beans,
    cut into 1-inch pieces
Fresh basil sprig and
    carrot ribbons
    (optional)

PREHEAT oven to 350°F. Spray 13×9-inch baking dish with nonstick cooking spray.

SPREAD almonds in single layer on baking sheet. Bake 5 minutes or until golden brown, stirring frequently.

MELT margarine in large skillet over medium-high heat. Add barley, chopped carrots, onions, celery and garlic; cook and stir 2 minutes or until onions are tender. Remove from heat. Stir in ham, almonds, dried basil, oregano and pepper. Pour into prepared dish.

POUR broth into medium saucepan; bring to a boil over high heat. Pour over barley mixture.

COVER tightly with foil and bake 20 minutes. Remove from oven; stir in green beans. Bake, covered, 30 minutes or until barley is tender. Garnish with fresh basil and carrot ribbons, if desired.

Makes 8 servings

Nutrients per Serving: Calories: 232, Total Fat: 7 g, Protein: 19 g, Carbohydrate: 27 g, Cholesterol: 32 mg, Sodium: 666 mg, Dietary Fiber: 5 g Dietary Exchanges: Vegetable: 1, Bread: 1½, Meat: 2

Hearty Biscuit-Topped Steak Pie

1½ pounds top round steak, cooked and cut into 1-inch cubes

1 package (9 ounces) frozen baby carrots

1 package (9 ounces) frozen peas and pearl onions

1 large baking potato, cooked, peeled and cut into ½-inch pieces

1 jar (18 ounces) home-style brown gravy

½ teaspoon dried thyme leaves

½ teaspoon black pepper

1 can (12 ounces) refrigerated flaky buttermilk biscuits

PREHEAT oven to 375°F. Spray 11×7-inch baking dish with nonstick cooking spray.

COMBINE steak, frozen vegetables and potato in prepared dish. Stir in gravy, thyme and pepper.

BAKE, uncovered, 40 minutes. Remove from oven. *Increase oven temperature to 400°F.* Top with biscuits and bake 8 to 10 minutes or until biscuits are golden brown.   *Makes 6 servings*

Nutrients per Serving: Calories: 413, Total Fat: 14 g, Protein: 34 g, Carbohydrate: 37 g, Cholesterol: 58 mg, Sodium: 1029 mg, Dietary Fiber: 2 g Dietary Exchanges: Vegetable: 1, Bread: 2, Meat: 3½, Fat: 1

Cook's Nook

This casserole can be prepared with leftovers of almost any kind. Other steaks, roast beef, stew meat, pork, lamb or chicken can be substituted for round steak; adjust gravy flavor to complement meat. Red potatoes can be used in place of baking potato. Choose your favorite vegetable combination as a substitute for the peas, onions and carrots.

Family-Style Hot Dogs with Red Beans and Rice

1 tablespoon vegetable oil
1 medium onion, chopped
½ medium green bell
    pepper, chopped
2 cloves garlic, minced
1 can (14 ounces) red
    kidney beans, drained
    and rinsed
1 can (14 ounces) Great
    Northern beans,
    drained and rinsed

½ pound beef hot dogs, cut
    into ¼-inch-thick slices
1 cup uncooked instant
    brown rice
1 cup vegetable broth
¼ cup ketchup
¼ cup packed brown sugar
3 tablespoons dark
    molasses
1 tablespoon Dijon mustard
    Zucchini ribbons (optional)

PREHEAT oven to 350°F. Spray 13×9-inch baking dish with nonstick cooking spray.

HEAT oil in Dutch oven over medium-high heat until hot. Add onion, pepper and garlic; cook and stir 2 minutes or until onion is tender.

ADD beans, hot dogs, rice, broth, ketchup, sugar, molasses and mustard to vegetables; stir to combine. Pour into prepared dish.

COVER tightly with foil and bake 30 minutes or until rice is tender. Garnish with zucchini, if desired.   *Makes 6 servings*

Nutrients per Serving: Calories: 475, Total Fat: 15 g, Protein: 18 g, Carbohydrate: 72 g, Cholesterol: 23 mg, Sodium: 714 mg, Dietary Fiber: 7 g
Dietary Exchanges: Vegetable: 1, Bread: 3, Meat: 1, Fat: 4

Cook's Nook

Smoked sausage can be substituted for hot dogs. Cut sausage into ¼-inch-thick slices and add with beans.

Beefy Nacho Crescent Bake

1 pound lean ground beef
½ cup chopped onion
¼ teaspoon salt
⅛ teaspoon black pepper
1 tablespoon chili powder
1 teaspoon ground cumin
1 teaspoon dried oregano
    leaves
1 can (11 ounces)
    condensed nacho
    cheese soup, undiluted

1 cup milk
1 can (8 ounces)
    refrigerated crescent
    roll dough
¼ cup (1 ounce) shredded
    Cheddar cheese
Chopped fresh cilantro
    (optional)
Salsa (optional)

PREHEAT oven to 375°F. Spray 13×9-inch baking dish with nonstick cooking spray.

PLACE beef and onion in large skillet; sprinkle with salt and pepper. Brown beef over medium-high heat until no longer pink, stirring to separate beef. Drain fat. Stir in chili powder, cumin and oregano. Cook and stir 2 minutes; remove from heat.

COMBINE soup and milk in medium bowl, stirring until smooth. Pour soup mixture into prepared dish, spreading evenly.

SEPARATE crescent dough into 4 rectangles; press perforations together firmly. Roll out each rectangle to 8×4 inches. Cut each rectangle in half crosswise to form 8 (4-inch) squares.

SPOON about ¼ cup beef mixture in center of each square. Lift 4 corners of dough up over filling to meet in center; pinch and twist firmly to seal. Place squares in dish.

BAKE, uncovered, 20 to 25 minutes or until crusts are golden brown. Sprinkle cheese over squares. Bake 5 minutes or until cheese melts. To serve, spoon soup mixture over each serving; sprinkle with cilantro, if desired. Serve with salsa, if desired.

Makes 4 servings

Nutrients per Serving: Calories: 564, Total Fat: 35 g, Protein: 31 g, Carbohydrate: 35 g, Cholesterol: 93 mg, Sodium: 1260 mg, Dietary Fiber: 3 g Dietary Exchanges: Bread: 2, Meat: 3, Fat: 5½

Reuben Noodle Bake

8 ounces uncooked egg
   noodles
5 ounces thinly sliced
   corned beef
1 can (14½ ounces)
   sauerkraut with
   caraway seeds, drained
2 cups (8 ounces) shredded
   Swiss cheese
½ cup Thousand Island
   dressing

½ cup milk
1 tablespoon prepared
   mustard
2 slices pumpernickel
   bread
1 tablespoon margarine or
   butter, melted
Red onion slices
   (optional)

PREHEAT oven to 350°F. Spray 13×9-inch baking dish with nonstick cooking spray.

COOK noodles according to package directions until al dente. Drain.

Meanwhile, **CUT** corned beef into bite-size pieces. Combine noodles, corned beef, sauerkraut and cheese in large bowl. Pour into prepared dish.

COMBINE dressing, milk and mustard in small bowl. Spoon dressing mixture evenly over noodle mixture.

TEAR bread into large pieces. Process in food processor or blender until crumbs are formed. Combine bread crumbs and margarine in small bowl; sprinkle evenly over casserole.

BAKE, uncovered, 25 to 30 minutes or until heated through. Garnish with red onion, if desired.   *Makes 6 servings*

Serving Suggestion: Serve with a mixed green salad.

Nutrients per Serving: Calories: 456, Total Fat: 22 g, Protein: 23 g, Carbohydrate: 41 g, Cholesterol: 102 mg, Sodium: 1331 mg, Dietary Fiber: 1 g Dietary Exchanges: Vegetable: 1, Bread: 2½, Meat: 2, Fat: 3

Spicy Manicotti

3 cups ricotta cheese
1 cup grated Parmesan cheese, divided
2 eggs, lightly beaten
2½ tablespoons chopped fresh parsley
1 teaspoon dried Italian seasoning
½ teaspoon garlic powder
½ teaspoon salt
½ teaspoon black pepper

1 pound spicy Italian sausage, casing removed
1 can (28 ounces) crushed tomatoes in purée, undrained
1 jar (26 ounces) marinara or spaghetti sauce
8 ounces uncooked manicotti noodles

PREHEAT oven to 375°F. Spray 13×9-inch baking dish with nonstick cooking spray.

COMBINE ricotta cheese, ¾ cup Parmesan cheese, eggs, parsley, Italian seasoning, garlic powder, salt and pepper in medium bowl; set aside.

CRUMBLE sausage into large skillet; brown over medium-high heat until no longer pink, stirring to separate sausage. Drain sausage on paper towels; drain fat from skillet.

ADD tomatoes with juice and marinara sauce to same skillet; bring to a boil over high heat. Reduce heat to low; simmer, uncovered, 10 minutes. Pour about one third of sauce into prepared dish.

STUFF each uncooked noodle with about ½ cup cheese mixture. Place in dish. Top noodles with sausage; pour remaining sauce over noodles.

COVER tightly with foil and bake 50 minutes to 1 hour or until noodles are tender. Let stand 5 minutes before serving. Serve with remaining ¼ cup Parmesan cheese.   *Makes 8 servings*

Nutrients per Serving: Calories: 610, Total Fat: 38 g, Protein: 30 g, Carbohydrate: 38 g, Cholesterol: 154 mg, Sodium: 1660 mg, Dietary Fiber: 4 g
Dietary Exchanges: Vegetable: 2, Bread: 2, Meat: 3, Fat: 5½

Menu

Spicy Manicotti

Tossed Salad with
Vinaigrette Dressing

Garlic Bread

Italian Ice

Coffee

Pork Chops and Apple Stuffing

6 (¾-inch-thick) boneless
    pork loin chops (about
    1½ pounds)
¼ teaspoon salt
⅛ teaspoon black pepper
1 tablespoon vegetable oil
1 small onion, chopped
2 ribs celery, chopped
2 Granny Smith apples,
    peeled, cored and
    coarsely chopped
    (about 2 cups)

1 can (14½ ounces)
    reduced-sodium
    chicken broth
1 can (10¾ ounces)
    condensed cream of
    celery soup, undiluted
¼ cup dry white wine
6 cups herb-seasoned
    stuffing cubes

PREHEAT oven to 375°F. Spray 13×9-inch baking dish with nonstick cooking spray.

SPRINKLE both sides of pork chops with salt and pepper. Heat oil in large deep skillet over medium-high heat until hot. Add pork chops and cook until browned on both sides, turning once. Remove from skillet; set aside.

ADD onion and celery to same skillet. Cook and stir 3 minutes or until onion is tender. Add apples; cook and stir 1 minute. Add broth, soup and wine; stir until smooth. Bring to a simmer; remove from heat. Stir in stuffing cubes until evenly moistened.

POUR stuffing mixture into prepared dish, spreading evenly. Place pork chops on top of stuffing; pour any accumulated juices over pork chops.

COVER tightly with foil and bake 30 to 40 minutes or until pork chops are juicy and barely pink in centers.   *Makes 6 servings*

Serving Suggestion: Serve with a mixed green salad.

Nutrients per Serving: Calories: 373, Total Fat: 15 g, Protein: 21 g, Carbohydrate: 38 g, Cholesterol: 59 mg, Sodium: 935 mg, Dietary Fiber: 2 g Dietary Exchanges: Vegetable: 1, Fruit: 1, Bread: 1, Meat: 2½, Fat: 2

Beef Stroganoff Casserole

1 pound lean ground beef
¼ teaspoon salt
⅛ teaspoon black pepper
1 teaspoon vegetable oil
8 ounces sliced
    mushrooms
1 large onion, chopped
3 cloves garlic, minced
¼ cup dry white wine
1 can (10¾ ounces)
    condensed cream of
    mushroom soup,
    undiluted

½ cup sour cream
1 tablespoon Dijon mustard
4 cups cooked egg noodles
    Chopped fresh parsley
    (optional)
    Radish slices and fresh
    Italian parsley sprigs
    (optional)

PREHEAT oven to 350°F. Spray 13×9-inch baking dish with nonstick cooking spray.

PLACE beef in large skillet; sprinkle with salt and pepper. Brown beef over medium-high heat until no longer pink, stirring to separate beef. Drain fat from skillet; set aside beef.

HEAT oil in same skillet over medium-high heat until hot. Add mushrooms, onion and garlic; cook and stir 2 minutes or until onion is tender. Add wine. Reduce heat to medium-low and simmer 3 minutes. Remove from heat; stir in soup, sour cream and mustard until well combined. Return beef to skillet.

PLACE noodles in prepared dish. Pour beef mixture over noodles; stir until noodles are well coated.

BAKE, uncovered, 30 minutes or until heated through. Sprinkle with chopped parsley, if desired. Garnish with radish and parsley sprigs, if desired.

Makes 6 servings

Nutrients per Serving: Calories: 419, Total Fat: 20 g, Protein: 21 g, Carbohydrate: 36 g, Cholesterol: 91 mg, Sodium: 596 mg, Dietary Fiber: 3 g
Dietary Exchanges: Vegetable: 1, Bread: 2, Meat: 2, Fat: 3

Chicken & Turkey

Turkey & Green Bean Casserole

¼ cup slivered almonds
1 package (7 ounces) herb-seasoned stuffing cubes
¾ cup reduced-sodium chicken broth
1 can (10¾ ounces) condensed cream of mushroom soup, undiluted
¼ cup milk or half-and-half

¼ teaspoon black pepper
1 package (10 ounces) frozen French-style green beans, thawed and drained
2 cups diced cooked turkey or chicken (about ¾ pound)
Red bell pepper slices and fresh Italian parsley (optional)

PREHEAT oven to 350°F. Spray 11×7-inch baking dish with nonstick cooking spray. Spread almonds in single layer on baking sheet. Bake 5 minutes or until golden brown, stirring frequently. Set aside.

ADD stuffing to prepared dish; drizzle with broth. Stir to coat stuffing with broth. Combine soup, milk and black pepper in large bowl; stir in green beans and turkey. Spoon over stuffing; top with almonds.

BAKE, uncovered, 30 to 35 minutes or until heated through. Garnish with bell pepper and Italian parsley, if desired.   *Makes 4 servings*

Tip: Buying sliced turkey from the deli counter at your supermarket is a great way to save time when preparing a casserole. Just dice the turkey and add it to the casserole.

Nutrients per Serving: Calories: 403, Total Fat: 12 g, Protein: 22 g, Carbohydrate: 53 g, Cholesterol: 45 mg, Sodium: 1988 mg, Dietary Fiber: 2 g Dietary Exchanges: Vegetable: 1, Bread: 3, Meat: 1½, Fat: 2

Coq au Vin

½ cup all-purpose flour
1¼ teaspoons salt
¾ teaspoon black pepper
3½ pounds chicken pieces
2 tablespoons margarine or butter
8 ounces mushrooms, cut in half if large
4 cloves garlic, minced
¾ cup chicken broth

¾ cup dry red wine
2 teaspoons dried thyme leaves
1½ pounds red potatoes, quartered
2 cups frozen pearl onions (about 8 ounces)
Chopped fresh parsley (optional)

PREHEAT oven to 350°F.

COMBINE flour, salt and pepper in large resealable plastic food storage bag. Add chicken, two pieces at a time, and seal bag. Shake to coat chicken; remove chicken and set aside. Repeat with remaining pieces. Reserve remaining flour mixture.

MELT margarine in ovenproof Dutch oven over medium-high heat. Arrange chicken in single layer in Dutch oven and cook 3 minutes per side or until browned. Transfer to plate; set aside. Repeat with remaining pieces.

ADD mushrooms and garlic to Dutch oven; cook and stir 2 minutes. Sprinkle reserved flour mixture over mushroom mixture; cook and stir 1 minute. Add broth, wine and thyme; bring to a boil over high heat, stirring to scrape browned bits from bottom of Dutch oven. Add potatoes and onions; return to a boil. Remove from heat and place chicken in Dutch oven, partially covering chicken with broth mixture.

BAKE, covered, about 45 minutes or until chicken is no longer pink in centers, juices run clear and sauce is slightly thickened. Transfer chicken and vegetables to shallow bowls. Spoon sauce over chicken and vegetables. Sprinkle with parsley, if desired.

Makes 4 to 6 servings

Serving Suggestion: Serve with assorted fresh baked rolls.

Nutrients per Serving: Calories: 960, Total Fat: 37 g, Protein: 70 g, Carbohydrate: 79 g, Cholesterol: 198 mg, Sodium: 1154 mg, Dietary Fiber: 1 g Dietary Exchanges: Vegetable: 1, Bread: 5, Meat: 8, Fat: 3

Chicken Tetrazzini

8 ounces uncooked
vermicelli, broken in
half
1 can (10¾ ounces)
condensed cream of
mushroom soup,
undiluted
¼ cup half-and-half
3 tablespoons dry sherry
½ teaspoon salt
⅛ to ¼ teaspoon crushed
red pepper flakes
2 cups diced cooked
chicken (about
¾ pound)

1 cup frozen peas
½ cup grated Parmesan
cheese
1 cup fresh coarse bread
crumbs
2 tablespoons margarine or
butter, melted
Chopped fresh basil
(optional)
Lemon slices and lettuce
leaves (optional)

PREHEAT oven to 375°F. Spray 13×9-inch baking dish with nonstick cooking spray.

COOK pasta according to package directions until al dente. Drain.

Meanwhile, **COMBINE** soup, half-and-half, sherry, salt and pepper flakes in large bowl. Stir in chicken, peas and cheese. Add pasta to chicken mixture; stir until pasta is coated. Pour into prepared dish.

COMBINE bread crumbs and margarine in small bowl. Sprinkle evenly over casserole.

BAKE, uncovered, 25 to 30 minutes or until heated through and crumbs are golden brown. Sprinkle with basil, if desired. Garnish with lemon and lettuce, if desired.   *Makes 4 servings*

Nutrients per Serving: Calories: 614, Total Fat: 20 g, Protein: 40 g, Carbohydrate: 62 g, Cholesterol: 82 mg, Sodium: 2442 mg, Dietary Fiber: 2 g Dietary Exchanges: Bread: 4, Meat: 4, Fat: 2½

Turkey Meatball & Olive Casserole

2 cups uncooked rotini pasta
½ pound ground turkey
¼ cup dry bread crumbs
1 egg, slightly beaten
2 teaspoons dried minced onion
2 teaspoons white wine Worcestershire sauce
½ teaspoon dried Italian seasoning
½ teaspoon salt
⅛ teaspoon black pepper

1 tablespoon vegetable oil
1 can (10¾ ounces) condensed cream of celery soup, undiluted
½ cup low-fat plain yogurt
¾ cup pimiento-stuffed green olives, sliced
3 tablespoons Italian-style bread crumbs
1 tablespoon margarine or butter, melted
Paprika (optional)
Fresh herbs (optional)

PREHEAT oven to 350°F. Spray 2-quart round casserole with nonstick cooking spray.

COOK pasta according to package directions until al dente. Drain and set aside.

Meanwhile, **COMBINE** turkey, ¼ cup bread crumbs, egg, onion, Worcestershire, Italian seasoning, salt and pepper in medium bowl. Shape mixture into 1-inch meatballs.

HEAT oil in medium skillet over high heat until hot. Add meatballs in single layer; cook until lightly browned on all sides and still pink in centers, turning frequently. *Do not overcook.* Remove from skillet; drain on paper towels.

MIX soup and yogurt in large bowl. Add pasta, meatballs and olives; stir gently to combine. Transfer to prepared dish.

COMBINE 3 tablespoons bread crumbs and margarine in small bowl; sprinkle evenly over casserole. Sprinkle lightly with paprika, if desired.

BAKE, covered, 30 minutes. Uncover and bake 12 minutes or until meatballs are no longer pink in centers and casserole is hot and bubbly. Garnish with herbs, if desired.   *Makes 6 to 8 servings*

Nutrients per Serving: Calories: 337, Total Fat: 14 g, Protein: 15 g, Carbohydrate: 38 g, Cholesterol: 56 mg, Sodium: 1205 mg, Dietary Fiber: 1 g Dietary Exchanges: Bread: 2½, Meat: 1, Fat: 2

Chicken Pot Pie

2 tablespoons margarine or butter
¾ pound boneless skinless chicken breasts, cut into 1-inch pieces
¾ teaspoon salt
8 ounces fresh green beans, cut into 1-inch pieces (about 2 cups)
½ cup chopped red bell pepper
½ cup thinly sliced celery

3 tablespoons all-purpose flour
½ cup chicken broth
½ cup half-and-half
1 teaspoon dried thyme leaves
½ teaspoon rubbed sage
1 cup frozen pearl onions
½ cup frozen corn
Pastry for single-crust 10-inch pie

PREHEAT oven to 425°F. Spray 10-inch deep-dish pie plate with nonstick cooking spray.

MELT margarine in large deep skillet over medium-high heat. Add chicken; cook and stir 3 minutes or until no longer pink in centers. Sprinkle with salt. Add green beans, pepper and celery; cook and stir 3 minutes.

SPRINKLE flour evenly over chicken and vegetables; cook and stir 1 minute. Stir in broth, half-and-half, thyme and sage; bring to a boil over high heat. Reduce heat to low and simmer 3 minutes or until sauce is thickened. Stir in onions and corn. Return to a simmer; cook and stir 1 minute.

TRANSFER mixture to prepared pie plate. Place pie pastry over chicken mixture; turn pastry edge under and flute to seal. Cut 4 slits in pie pastry to allow steam to escape.

BAKE, uncovered, 20 minutes or until crust is light golden brown and chicken mixture is hot and bubbly. Let stand 5 minutes before serving.

Makes 6 servings

Nutrients per Serving: Calories: 285, Total Fat: 15 g, Protein: 16 g, Carbohydrate: 22 g, Cholesterol: 43 mg, Sodium: 583 mg, Dietary Fiber: 1 g
Dietary Exchanges: Vegetable: 1, Bread: 1, Meat: 1½, Fat: 2½

Indian-Spiced Chicken with Wild Rice

½ teaspoon salt
½ teaspoon ground cumin
½ teaspoon black pepper
¼ teaspoon ground cinnamon
¼ teaspoon ground turmeric
4 boneless skinless chicken breast halves (about 1 pound)
2 tablespoons olive oil
2 carrots, sliced

1 red bell pepper, chopped
1 rib celery, chopped
2 cloves garlic, minced
1 package (6 ounces) long grain and wild rice mix
2 cups reduced-sodium chicken broth
1 cup raisins
¼ cup sliced almonds
Red bell pepper slices (optional)

COMBINE salt, cumin, black pepper, cinnamon and turmeric in small bowl. Rub spice mixture on both sides of chicken. Place chicken on plate; cover and refrigerate 30 minutes.

PREHEAT oven to 350°F. Spray 9-inch square baking dish with nonstick cooking spray.

HEAT oil in large skillet over medium-high heat until hot. Add chicken; cook 2 minutes per side or until browned. Transfer to clean plate; set aside.

PLACE carrots, chopped bell pepper, celery and garlic in same skillet. Cook and stir 2 minutes. Add rice; cook 5 minutes, stirring frequently. Add broth and seasoning packet from rice mix; bring to a boil over high heat. Remove from heat; stir in raisins. Pour into prepared dish; place chicken on rice mixture. Sprinkle with almonds.

COVER tightly with foil and bake 35 minutes or until chicken is no longer pink in centers, juices run clear and rice is tender. Garnish with bell pepper slices, if desired. *Makes 4 servings*

Nutrients per Serving: Calories: 544, Total Fat: 17 g, Protein: 34 g, Carbohydrate: 67 g, Cholesterol: 69 mg, Sodium: 993 mg, Dietary Fiber: 4 g Dietary Exchanges: Vegetable: 2, Fruit: 2, Bread: 2, Meat: 3, Fat: 1½

Southern-Style Chicken and Greens

1 teaspoon salt
1 teaspoon paprika
½ teaspoon black pepper
3½ pounds chicken pieces
4 thick slices smoked bacon (4 ounces), cut crosswise into ¼-inch pieces
1 cup uncooked rice
1 can (14½ ounces) stewed tomatoes, undrained

1¼ cups chicken broth
2 cups packed coarsely chopped fresh collard or mustard greens or kale (3 to 4 ounces)
Tomato wedges and fresh Italian parsley (optional)

PREHEAT oven to 350°F.

COMBINE salt, paprika and pepper in small bowl. Sprinkle meaty side of chicken pieces with salt mixture; set aside.

PLACE bacon in ovenproof Dutch oven; cook over medium heat until crisp. Drain on paper towels. Reserve bacon fat. Heat bacon fat over medium-high heat until hot. Arrange chicken in single layer in Dutch oven and cook 3 minutes per side or until browned. Transfer to clean plate; set aside. Repeat with remaining pieces. Reserve 1 tablespoon bacon fat in Dutch oven; discard remaining bacon fat.

ADD rice to Dutch oven; cook and stir 1 minute. Add tomatoes with juice, broth, collard greens and half of bacon; bring to a boil over high heat. Remove from heat; arrange chicken over rice mixture.

BAKE, covered, about 40 minutes or until chicken is no longer pink in centers, juices run clear and most of liquid is absorbed. Let stand 5 minutes before serving. Transfer to serving platter; sprinkle with remaining bacon. Garnish with tomato and Italian parsley, if desired.

Makes 4 to 6 servings

Nutrients per Serving: Calories: 906, Total Fat: 45 g, Protein: 74 g, Carbohydrate: 46 g, Cholesterol: 224 mg, Sodium: 1744 mg, Dietary Fiber: 1 g Dietary Exchanges: Vegetable: 2, Bread: 2½, Meat: 9, Fat: 4

Menu

Southern-Style Chicken and Greens

Corn Bread

Peach Cobbler with
Vanilla Ice Cream

Iced Tea and Lemonade

Chicken Marsala

6 ounces uncooked broad egg noodles

½ cup Italian-style dry bread crumbs

1 teaspoon dried basil leaves

1 egg

1 teaspoon water

4 boneless skinless chicken breast halves

3 tablespoons olive oil, divided

¾ cup chopped onion

8 ounces cremini or button mushrooms, sliced

3 cloves garlic, minced

3 tablespoons all-purpose flour

1 can (14½ ounces) chicken broth

½ cup dry marsala wine

¾ teaspoon salt

¼ teaspoon black pepper
Chopped fresh parsley (optional)

PREHEAT oven to 375°F. Spray 11×7-inch baking dish with nonstick cooking spray. Cook noodles according to package directions until al dente. Drain and place in prepared dish.

Meanwhile, **COMBINE** bread crumbs and basil on shallow plate or pie plate. Beat egg with water on another shallow plate or pie plate. Dip chicken in egg mixture, letting excess drip off. Roll in crumb mixture, patting to coat. Heat 2 tablespoons oil in large skillet over medium-high heat until hot. Cook chicken 3 minutes per side or until browned. Transfer to clean plate; set aside.

HEAT remaining 1 tablespoon oil in same skillet over medium heat. Add onion; cook and stir 5 minutes. Add mushrooms and garlic; cook and stir 3 minutes. Sprinkle flour over onion mixture; cook and stir 1 minute. Add broth, wine, salt and pepper; bring to a boil over high heat. Cook and stir 5 minutes or until sauce thickens. Reserve ½ cup sauce. Pour remaining sauce over noodles; stir until noodles are well coated. Place chicken on top of noodles. Spoon reserved sauce over chicken.

BAKE, uncovered, 20 minutes or until chicken is no longer pink in centers. Sprinkle with parsley, if desired. *Makes 4 servings*

Nutrients per Serving: Calories: 539, Total Fat: 19 g, Protein: 39 g, Carbohydrate: 49 g, Cholesterol: 175 mg, Sodium: 1224 mg, Dietary Fiber: 1 g
Dietary Exchanges: Vegetable: 1, Bread: 3, Meat: 3, Fat: 3

Turkey and Biscuits

2 cans (10¾ ounces each) condensed cream of chicken soup, undiluted
¼ cup dry white wine
¼ teaspoon poultry seasoning
2 packages (8 ounces each) frozen cut asparagus, thawed

3 cups diced cooked turkey or chicken
Paprika (optional)
1 can (11 ounces) refrigerated flaky biscuits

PREHEAT oven to 350°F. Spray 13×9-inch baking dish with nonstick cooking spray.

COMBINE soup, wine and poultry seasoning in medium bowl.

ARRANGE asparagus in single layer in prepared dish. Place turkey evenly over asparagus. Spread soup mixture over turkey. Sprinkle lightly with paprika, if desired.

COVER tightly with foil and bake 20 minutes. Remove from oven. *Increase oven temperature to 425°F.* Top with biscuits and bake, uncovered, 8 to 10 minutes or until biscuits are golden brown.

Makes 6 servings

Nutrients per Serving: Calories: 369, Total Fat: 18 g, Protein: 18 g, Carbohydrate: 32 g, Cholesterol: 57 mg, Sodium: 1796 mg, Dietary Fiber: 2 g
Dietary Exchanges: Vegetable: 1, Bread: 1½, Meat: 2, Fat: 3

Cook's Nook

Poultry seasoning is a powdered herb blend of sage, thyme, marjoram, savory, onion, black pepper and celery seed.

Sweet & Sour Chicken and Rice

1 pound chicken tenders
1 can (8 ounces) pineapple chunks, drained and juice reserved
1 cup uncooked rice
2 carrots, thinly sliced
1 green bell pepper, cut into 1-inch pieces
1 large onion, chopped
3 cloves garlic, minced
1 can (14½ ounces) reduced-sodium chicken broth

⅓ cup soy sauce
3 tablespoons sugar
3 tablespoons cider vinegar
1 tablespoon dark sesame oil
1½ teaspoons ground ginger
¼ cup chopped peanuts (optional)
Chopped fresh cilantro (optional)

PREHEAT oven to 350°F. Spray 13×9-inch baking dish with nonstick cooking spray.

COMBINE chicken, pineapple, rice, carrots, pepper, onion and garlic in prepared dish.

PLACE broth, reserved pineapple juice, soy sauce, sugar, vinegar, sesame oil and ginger in small saucepan; bring to a boil over high heat. Remove from heat and pour over chicken mixture.

COVER tightly with foil and bake 40 to 50 minutes or until chicken is no longer pink in centers, juices run clear and rice is tender. Sprinkle with peanuts and cilantro, if desired.   *Makes 6 servings*

Nutrients per Serving: Calories: 309, Total Fat: 5 g, Protein: 21 g, Carbohydrate: 45 g, Cholesterol: 46 mg, Sodium: 983 mg, Dietary Fiber: 2 g Dietary Exchanges: Vegetable: 1, Fruit: ½, Bread: 2, Meat: 2

Artichoke-Olive Chicken Bake

1½ cups uncooked rotini pasta
1 tablespoon olive oil
1 medium onion, chopped
½ green bell pepper, chopped
2 cups shredded cooked chicken
1 can (14½ ounces) diced tomatoes with Italian-style herbs, undrained

1 can (14 ounces) artichoke hearts, drained and quartered
1 can (6 ounces) sliced black olives, drained
1 teaspoon dried Italian seasoning
2 cups (8 ounces) shredded mozzarella cheese
Fresh basil sprig (optional)

PREHEAT oven to 350°F. Spray 13×9-inch baking dish with nonstick cooking spray.

COOK pasta according to package directions until al dente. Drain and set aside.

Meanwhile, **HEAT** oil in large deep skillet over medium heat until hot. Add onion and pepper; cook and stir 1 minute. Add chicken, tomatoes with juice, pasta, artichokes, olives and Italian seasoning; mix until combined.

PLACE half of chicken mixture in prepared dish; sprinkle with half of cheese. Top with remaining chicken mixture and cheese.

BAKE, covered, 35 minutes or until hot and bubbly. Garnish with basil, if desired.   *Makes 8 servings*

Nutrients per Serving: Calories: 369, Total Fat: 18 g, Protein: 21 g, Carbohydrate: 34 g, Cholesterol: 43 mg, Sodium: 1497 mg, Dietary Fiber: 7 g
Dietary Exchanges: Vegetable: 3, Bread: 1, Meat: 2, Fat: 2½

Cook's Nook

Serve with crusty Italian or French bread and a tossed salad.

Roasted Chicken and Vegetables over Wild Rice

3½ pounds chicken pieces
¾ cup olive oil vinaigrette dressing, divided
1 tablespoon margarine or butter, melted
1 package (6 ounces) long grain and wild rice mix
1 can (13¾ ounces) reduced-sodium chicken broth
1 small eggplant, cut into 1-inch pieces
2 medium red potatoes, cut into 1-inch pieces
1 medium yellow squash, cut into 1-inch pieces
1 medium zucchini, cut into 1-inch pieces
1 medium red onion, cut into wedges
1 package (4 ounces) crumbled feta cheese with basil
Chopped fresh cilantro (optional)
Fresh thyme sprig (optional)

REMOVE skin from chicken; discard. Combine chicken and ½ cup dressing in large resealable plastic food storage bag. Seal bag and turn to coat. Refrigerate 30 minutes or overnight.

PREHEAT oven to 375°F. Coat bottom of 13×9-inch baking dish with margarine.

ADD rice and seasoning packet to prepared dish; stir in broth. Combine eggplant, potatoes, squash, zucchini and onion in large bowl. Place on top of rice mixture.

REMOVE chicken from bag and place on top of vegetables; discard marinade. Pour remaining ¼ cup dressing over chicken.

BAKE, uncovered, 45 minutes. Remove from oven and sprinkle with cheese. Bake 5 to 10 minutes or until chicken is no longer pink in centers, juices run clear and cheese is melted. Sprinkle with cilantro, if desired. Garnish with thyme, if desired.   *Makes 4 to 6 servings*

Nutrients per Serving: Calories: 858, Total Fat: 42 g, Protein: 47 g, Carbohydrate: 70 g, Cholesterol: 125 mg, Sodium: 1092 mg, Dietary Fiber: 1 g Dietary Exchanges: Vegetable: 2, Bread: 4, Meat: 4½, Fat: 6

Fish & Shellfish

Flounder Fillets over Zesty Lemon Rice

¼ cup margarine or butter
3 tablespoons fresh lemon juice
2 teaspoons chicken bouillon granules
½ teaspoon black pepper
1 cup cooked rice
1 package (10 ounces) frozen chopped broccoli, thawed

1 cup (4 ounces) shredded sharp Cheddar cheese
1 pound flounder fillets
½ teaspoon paprika
Lemon slices, lemon peel and fresh parsley (optional)

PREHEAT oven to 375°F. Spray 2-quart square casserole with nonstick cooking spray.

MELT margarine in small saucepan over medium heat. Add lemon juice, bouillon and pepper; cook and stir 2 minutes or until bouillon is dissolved.

COMBINE rice, broccoli, cheese and ¼ cup lemon sauce in medium bowl; spread on bottom of prepared dish. Place fillets on top of rice mixture. Pour remaining lemon sauce over fillets.

BAKE, uncovered, 20 minutes or until fish flakes easily when tested with fork. Sprinkle evenly with paprika. Garnish with lemon and parsley, if desired.   *Makes 6 servings*

Nutrients per Serving: Calories: 263, Total Fat: 12 g, Protein: 25 g, Carbohydrate: 12 g, Cholesterol: 61 mg, Sodium: 650 mg, Dietary Fiber: 1 g Dietary Exchanges: Vegetable: 1, Bread: ½, Meat: 3, Fat: 1

Tuna Noodle Casserole

7 ounces uncooked elbow macaroni

2 tablespoons margarine or butter

¾ cup chopped onion

½ cup thinly sliced celery

½ cup finely chopped red bell pepper

2 tablespoons all-purpose flour

1 teaspoon salt

⅛ teaspoon ground white pepper

1½ cups milk

1 can (6 ounces) albacore tuna in water, drained

½ cup grated Parmesan cheese, divided

Fresh dill sprigs (optional)

PREHEAT oven to 375°F. Spray 8-inch square baking dish with nonstick cooking spray.

COOK pasta according to package directions until al dente. Drain and set aside.

Meanwhile, **MELT** margarine in large deep skillet over medium heat. Add onion; cook and stir 3 minutes. Add celery and bell pepper; cook and stir 3 minutes. Sprinkle flour, salt and white pepper over vegetables; cook and stir 1 minute. Gradually stir in milk; cook and stir until thickened. Remove from heat.

ADD pasta, tuna and ¼ cup cheese to skillet; stir until pasta is well coated. Pour tuna mixture into prepared dish; sprinkle evenly with remaining ¼ cup cheese.

BAKE, uncovered, 20 to 25 minutes or until hot and bubbly. Garnish with dill, if desired. *Makes 4 servings*

Nutrients per Serving: Calories: 424, Total Fat: 12 g, Protein: 27 g, Carbohydrate: 50 g, Cholesterol: 29 mg, Sodium: 1038 mg, Dietary Fiber: 1 g Dietary Exchanges: Vegetable: 1, Bread: 3, Meat: 2, Fat: 1½

Cook's Nook

Serve with spinach salad and warm biscuits.

Jambalaya

1 teaspoon vegetable oil

½ pound smoked deli ham, cubed

½ pound smoked sausage, cut into ¼-inch-thick slices

1 large onion, chopped

1 large green bell pepper, chopped (about 1½ cups)

3 ribs celery, chopped (about 1 cup)

3 cloves garlic, minced

1 can (28 ounces) diced tomatoes, undrained

1 can (10½ ounces) chicken broth

1 cup uncooked rice

1 tablespoon Worcestershire sauce

1 teaspoon dried thyme leaves

1 teaspoon salt

½ teaspoon black pepper

¼ teaspoon ground red pepper

1 package (12 ounces) frozen ready-to-cook shrimp, thawed

Fresh chives (optional)

PREHEAT oven to 350°F. Spray 13×9-inch baking dish with nonstick cooking spray.

HEAT oil in large skillet over medium-high heat until hot. Add ham and sausage. Cook and stir 5 minutes or until sausage is lightly browned on both sides. Remove from skillet and place in prepared dish. Place onion, bell pepper, celery and garlic in same skillet; cook and stir 3 minutes. Add to sausage mixture.

COMBINE tomatoes with juice, broth, rice, Worcestershire, thyme, salt and black and red peppers in same skillet; bring to a boil over high heat. Reduce heat to low and simmer 3 minutes. Pour over sausage mixture and stir until combined.

COVER tightly with foil and bake 45 minutes or until rice is almost tender. Remove from oven; place shrimp on top of rice mixture. Bake, uncovered, 10 minutes or until shrimp are pink and opaque. Garnish with chives, if desired.   *Makes 8 servings*

Nutrients per Serving: Calories: 285, Total Fat: 10 g, Protein: 20 g, Carbohydrate: 29 g, Cholesterol: 104 mg, Sodium: 1485 mg, Dietary Fiber: 1 g Dietary Exchanges: Vegetable: 2, Bread: 1, Meat: 2, Fat: 1

Pasta with Salmon and Dill

6 ounces uncooked mafalda pasta
1 tablespoon olive oil
2 ribs celery, sliced
1 small red onion, chopped
1 can (10¾ ounces) condensed cream of celery soup, undiluted
¼ cup reduced-fat mayonnaise
¼ cup dry white wine

3 tablespoons chopped fresh parsley
1 teaspoon dried dill weed
1 can (7½ ounces) pink salmon, drained
½ cup dry bread crumbs
1 tablespoon margarine or butter, melted
Fresh dill sprigs and red onion slices (optional)

PREHEAT oven to 350°F. Spray 1-quart square baking dish with nonstick cooking spray.

COOK pasta according to package directions until al dente. Drain and set aside.

Meanwhile, **HEAT** oil in medium skillet over medium-high heat until hot. Add celery and chopped onion; cook and stir 2 minutes or until vegetables are tender. Set aside.

COMBINE soup, mayonnaise, wine, parsley and dill weed in large bowl. Stir in pasta, vegetables and salmon until pasta is well coated. Pour salmon mixture into prepared dish.

COMBINE bread crumbs and margarine in small bowl; sprinkle evenly over casserole.

BAKE, uncovered, 25 minutes or until hot and bubbly. Garnish with fresh dill and red onion slices, if desired.   *Makes 4 servings*

Nutrients per Serving: Calories: 468, Total Fat: 20 g, Protein: 18 g, Carbohydrate: 51 g, Cholesterol: 25 mg, Sodium: 988 mg, Dietary Fiber: 1 g
Dietary Exchanges: Vegetable: 1, Bread: 3, Meat: 1, Fat: 4

Cook's Nook

Mafalda pasta is a broad, flat noodle with rippled edges that is similar to a small lasagna noodle.

Menu

Pasta with Salmon and Dill

Buttered Steamed Carrots

Focaccia Bread

White Wine

Tuna Pot Pie

1 tablespoon margarine or butter
1 small onion, chopped
1 can (10¾ ounces) condensed cream of potato soup, undiluted
¼ cup milk
½ teaspoon dried thyme leaves
¼ teaspoon salt
⅛ teaspoon black pepper
2 cans (6 ounces each) albacore tuna in water, drained

1 package (16 ounces) frozen vegetable medley (such as broccoli, green beans, pearl onions and red peppers), thawed
2 tablespoons chopped fresh parsley
1 can (8 ounces) refrigerated crescent roll dough

PREHEAT oven to 350°F. Spray 11×7-inch baking dish with nonstick cooking spray.

MELT margarine in large skillet over medium heat. Add onion; cook and stir 2 minutes or until onion is tender. Add soup, milk, thyme, salt and pepper; cook and stir 3 to 4 minutes or until thick and bubbly. Stir in tuna, vegetables and parsley. Pour mixture into prepared dish.

UNROLL crescent roll dough and separate into triangles. Place triangles over tuna mixture without overlapping dough.

BAKE, uncovered, 20 minutes or until triangles are golden brown. Let stand 5 minutes before serving.   *Makes 6 servings*

Nutrients per Serving: Calories: 312, Total Fat: 13 g, Protein: 21 g, Carbohydrate: 31 g, Cholesterol: 27 mg, Sodium: 1076 mg, Dietary Fiber: 1 g Dietary Exchanges: Vegetable: 2, Bread: 1½, Meat: 2, Fat: 1

Cook's Nook

Create an exciting recipe by substituting a new vegetable medley for the one listed. Enjoy the results!

Creamy "Crab" Fettuccine

1 pound imitation crabmeat sticks

6 ounces uncooked fettuccine

3 tablespoons margarine or butter, divided

1 small onion, chopped

2 ribs celery, chopped

½ medium red bell pepper, chopped

2 cloves garlic, minced

1 cup reduced-fat sour cream

1 cup reduced-fat mayonnaise

1 cup (4 ounces) shredded sharp Cheddar cheese

2 tablespoons chopped fresh parsley

¼ teaspoon salt

⅛ teaspoon black pepper

½ cup cornflake crumbs

Fresh chives (optional)

PREHEAT oven to 350°F. Spray 2-quart square baking dish with nonstick cooking spray.

CUT crabmeat into bite-size pieces; set aside.

COOK pasta according to package directions until al dente. Drain and set aside.

Meanwhile, **MELT** 1 tablespoon margarine in large skillet over medium-high heat. Add onion, celery, bell pepper and garlic; cook and stir 2 minutes or until vegetables are tender. Set aside.

COMBINE sour cream, mayonnaise, cheese, parsley, salt and black pepper in large bowl. Add crabmeat, pasta and vegetable mixture, stirring gently to combine. Pour into prepared dish.

MELT remaining 2 tablespoons margarine. Combine cornflake crumbs and margarine in small bowl; sprinkle evenly over casserole.

BAKE, uncovered, 30 minutes or until hot and bubbly. Garnish with chives, if desired.   *Makes 6 servings*

Nutrients per Serving: Calories: 471, Total Fat: 24 g, Protein: 20 g, Carbohydrate: 42 g, Cholesterol: 51 mg, Sodium: 1140 mg, Dietary Fiber: 1 g
Dietary Exchanges: Vegetable: 1, Bread: 2½, Meat: 1½, Fat: 4

Vegetables & Sides

Mexican Tortilla Stack-Ups

1 tablespoon vegetable oil
½ cup chopped onion
1 can (15 ounces) black beans, drained and rinsed
1 can (14½ ounces) Mexican- or Italian-style diced tomatoes, undrained
1 cup frozen corn

1 envelope (1¼ ounces) taco seasoning mix
6 (6-inch) corn tortillas
2 cups (8 ounces) shredded Cheddar cheese with taco seasonings
1 cup water
Sour cream (optional)
Sliced black olives (optional)

PREHEAT oven to 350°F. Spray 13×9-inch baking dish with nonstick cooking spray.

HEAT oil in large skillet over medium-high heat until hot. Add onion; cook and stir 3 minutes or until tender. Add beans, tomatoes with juice, corn and taco seasoning mix. Bring to a boil over high heat. Reduce heat to low and simmer 5 minutes.

PLACE 2 tortillas side by side in prepared dish. Top each tortilla with about ½ cup bean mixture. Sprinkle evenly with one third of cheese. Repeat layers twice, creating 2 tortilla stacks each 3 tortillas high.

POUR water along sides of tortillas.

COVER tightly with foil and bake 30 to 35 minutes or until heated through. Cut into wedges to serve. Serve with sour cream and olives, if desired.
Makes 6 servings

Nutrients per Serving: Calories: 352, Total Fat: 16 g, Protein: 19 g, Carbohydrate: 38 g, Cholesterol: 40 mg, Sodium: 1031 mg, Dietary Fiber: 5 g Dietary Exchanges: Vegetable: 1, Bread: 2, Meat: 2, Fat: 1½

Easy Cheesy Lasagna

2 tablespoons olive oil

3 small zucchini, quartered lengthwise and thinly sliced crosswise

1 package (8 ounces) mushrooms, thinly sliced

1 medium onion, chopped

5 cloves garlic, minced

2 containers (15 ounces each) reduced-fat ricotta cheese

¼ cup grated Parmesan cheese

2 eggs

½ teaspoon dried Italian seasoning

¼ teaspoon garlic salt

⅛ teaspoon black pepper

1 can (28 ounces) crushed tomatoes in purée, undrained

1 jar (26 ounces) spaghetti sauce

1 package (16 ounces) lasagna noodles, uncooked

4 cups (16 ounces) shredded mozzarella cheese

PREHEAT oven to 375°F. Spray 13×9-inch baking dish or lasagna pan with nonstick cooking spray. Heat oil in large skillet over medium heat until hot. Add zucchini, mushrooms, onion and garlic; cook and stir 5 minutes.

COMBINE ricotta cheese, Parmesan cheese, eggs, Italian seasoning, garlic salt and pepper in medium bowl. Combine tomatoes and spaghetti sauce in another medium bowl.

SPREAD about ¾ cup tomato mixture in prepared dish. Place layer of uncooked noodles over tomato mixture, overlapping noodles. Spread half of vegetable mixture over noodles; top with half of ricotta cheese mixture. Sprinkle 1 cup mozzarella cheese over ricotta cheese mixture. Top with second layer of noodles. Spread about 1 cup tomato mixture over noodles. Top with remaining vegetable and ricotta cheese mixtures. Sprinkle with 1 cup mozzarella cheese. Top with third layer of noodles. Spread remaining tomato mixture over noodles. Sprinkle with remaining 2 cups mozzarella cheese.

COVER tightly with foil and bake 1 hour or until noodles in center are soft. Uncover; bake 5 minutes or until cheese is melted. Cover and let stand 15 minutes before serving.   *Makes 10 to 12 servings*

Nutrients per Serving: Calories: 453, Total Fat: 19 g, Protein: 28 g, Carbohydrate: 45 g, Cholesterol: 96 mg, Sodium: 1072 mg, Dietary Fiber: 6 g Dietary Exchanges: Vegetable: 2, Bread: 2, Meat: 3, Fat: 2

Greek Spinach and Feta Pie

⅓ cup butter, melted and
　divided
2 eggs
1 package (10 ounces)
　frozen chopped
　spinach, thawed and
　squeezed dry
1 container (15 ounces)
　ricotta cheese

1 package (4 ounces)
　crumbled feta cheese
¾ teaspoon finely grated
　lemon peel
¼ teaspoon black pepper
⅛ teaspoon ground nutmeg
1 package (16 ounces)
　frozen phyllo dough,
　thawed

PREHEAT oven to 350°F. Brush 13×9-inch baking dish lightly with butter.

BEAT eggs in medium bowl. Stir in spinach, ricotta cheese, feta cheese, lemon peel, pepper and nutmeg. Set aside.

CUT 8 sheets of phyllo dough in half crosswise, forming 16 rectangles about 13×8½ inches each. Cover dough with damp cloth or plastic wrap while assembling pie. Reserve remaining dough for another use.

PLACE 1 piece of dough in prepared dish; brush top lightly with butter. Top with another piece of dough and brush lightly with butter. Continue layering with 6 pieces of dough, brushing each piece lightly with butter. Spoon spinach mixture evenly over dough. Top spinach mixture with piece of dough; brush lightly with butter. Repeat layering with remaining 7 pieces of dough, brushing each piece lightly with butter.

BAKE, uncovered, 35 to 40 minutes or until golden brown.

Makes 6 servings

Serving Suggestion: Serve with cantaloupe slices and cherries.

Nutrients per Serving: Calories: 525, Total Fat: 30 g, Protein: 20 g,
Carbohydrate: 45 g, Cholesterol: 151 mg, Sodium: 795 mg, Dietary Fiber: trace
Dietary Exchanges: Vegetable: 1, Bread: 2½, Meat: 2, Fat: 4½

Baked Tomato Risotto

···

2 medium zucchini
1 jar (28 ounces) spaghetti
    sauce
1 can (14 ounces) chicken
    broth
1 can (4 ounces) sliced
    mushrooms

1 cup arborio rice
2 cups (8 ounces) shredded
    mozzarella cheese
Yellow bell pepper slices
    (optional)

PREHEAT oven to 350°F. Spray 3-quart oval casserole with nonstick cooking spray.

CUT zucchini lengthwise in half. Cut crosswise into ¼-inch-thick slices. Combine spaghetti sauce, broth, zucchini, mushrooms and rice in prepared dish.

BAKE, covered, 30 minutes. Remove from oven and stir casserole. Cover and bake 15 to 20 minutes or until rice is tender. Remove from oven; sprinkle evenly with cheese. Bake, uncovered, 5 minutes or until cheese is melted. Garnish with yellow pepper, if desired.

Makes 6 servings

Nutrients per Serving: Calories: 350, Total Fat: 9 g, Protein: 15 g, Carbohydrate: 51 g, Cholesterol: 27 mg, Sodium: 977 mg, Dietary Fiber: 1 g Dietary Exchanges: Vegetable: 2, Bread: 2½, Meat: 1½, Fat: ½

Cook's Nook

Arborio is an Italian-grown short-grain rice that has large, plump grains. It is used in risotto dishes because its high starch content produces a creamy texture and it can absorb more liquid than long-grain rice.

Italian Three-Cheese Macaroni

2 cups uncooked elbow macaroni

4 tablespoons margarine or butter

3 tablespoons all-purpose flour

1 teaspoon dried Italian seasoning

½ to 1 teaspoon black pepper

½ teaspoon salt

2 cups milk

¾ cup (3 ounces) shredded Cheddar cheese

¼ cup grated Parmesan cheese

1 can (14½ ounces) diced tomatoes, drained

1 cup (4 ounces) shredded mozzarella cheese

½ cup dry bread crumbs Fresh chives and oregano sprig (optional)

PREHEAT oven to 350°F. Spray 2-quart round casserole with nonstick cooking spray.

COOK pasta according to package directions until al dente. Drain and set aside.

Meanwhile, **MELT** margarine in medium saucepan over medium heat. Add flour, Italian seasoning, pepper and salt, stirring until smooth. Gradually add milk, stirring constantly until slightly thickened. Add Cheddar and Parmesan cheeses; stir until cheeses melt.

LAYER pasta, tomatoes and cheese sauce in prepared dish. Repeat layers.

COMBINE mozzarella cheese and bread crumbs in small bowl. Sprinkle evenly over casserole. Spray bread crumb mixture several times with cooking spray.

BAKE, covered, 30 minutes or until hot and bubbly. Uncover and bake 5 minutes or until top is golden brown. Garnish with chives and oregano, if desired.

Makes 4 servings

Nutrients per Serving: Calories: 621, Total Fat: 26 g, Protein: 29 g, Carbohydrate: 67 g, Cholesterol: 41 mg, Sodium: 1303 mg, Dietary Fiber: trace Dietary Exchanges: Milk: ½, Vegetable: 2, Bread: 3½, Meat: 2, Fat: 3½

Spinach-Cheese Pasta Casserole

8 ounces uncooked pasta
shells
2 eggs
1 cup ricotta cheese
1 jar (26 ounces) marinara
sauce
1 teaspoon salt

1 package (10 ounces)
frozen chopped
spinach, thawed and
squeezed dry
1 cup (4 ounces) shredded
mozzarella cheese
¼ cup grated Parmesan
cheese

PREHEAT oven to 350°F. Spray 1½-quart round casserole with nonstick cooking spray.

COOK pasta according to package directions until al dente. Drain.

Meanwhile, **WHISK** eggs in large bowl until blended. Add ricotta cheese; stir until combined. Stir pasta, marinara sauce and salt in large bowl until pasta is well coated. Pour pasta mixture into prepared dish. Top with ricotta mixture and spinach. Sprinkle mozzarella and Parmesan cheeses evenly over casserole.

BAKE, covered, 30 minutes. Uncover and bake 15 minutes or until hot and bubbly.   *Makes 6 to 8 servings*

Nutrients per Serving: Calories: 392, Total Fat: 16 g, Protein: 21 g, Carbohydrate: 40 g, Cholesterol: 106 mg, Sodium: 1072 mg, Dietary Fiber: 2 g Dietary Exchanges: Vegetable: 2, Bread: 2, Meat: 2, Fat: 2

Potatoes au Gratin

1½ pounds small red
    potatoes
6 tablespoons margarine or
    butter, divided
3 tablespoons all-purpose
    flour
½ teaspoon salt
¼ teaspoon ground white
    pepper

1½ cups milk
1 cup (4 ounces) shredded
    Cheddar cheese
4 green onions, thinly
    sliced
¾ cup cracker crumbs

PREHEAT oven to 350°F. Spray 1-quart round casserole with nonstick cooking spray.

PLACE potatoes in 2-quart saucepan; add enough water to cover potatoes. Bring to a boil over high heat. Cook, uncovered, about 10 minutes or until partially done. *Potatoes should still be firm in center.* Drain and rinse in cold water until potatoes are cool. Drain and set aside.

Meanwhile, **MELT** 4 tablespoons margarine in medium saucepan over medium heat. Add flour, salt and pepper, stirring until smooth. Gradually add milk, stirring constantly until sauce is thickened. Add cheese, stirring until cheese is melted.

CUT potatoes crosswise into ¼-inch-thick slices. Layer one third of potatoes in prepared dish. Top with one third of onions and one third of cheese sauce. Repeat layers twice, ending with cheese sauce.

MELT remaining 2 tablespoons margarine. Combine cracker crumbs and margarine in small bowl. Sprinkle evenly over casserole.

BAKE, uncovered, 35 to 40 minutes or until hot and bubbly and potatoes are tender.   *Makes 4 to 6 servings*

Nutrients per Serving: Calories: 634, Total Fat: 24 g, Protein: 18 g, Carbohydrate: 87 g, Cholesterol: 22 mg, Sodium: 708 mg, Dietary Fiber: trace Dietary Exchanges: Bread: 6, Fat: 4½

Menu

Roast Beef

Potatoes au Gratin

Steamed Broccoli

Assorted Rolls

Apple Crisp with
Vanilla Ice Cream

Green Beans with Blue Cheese and Roasted Red Peppers

1 bag (20 ounces) frozen
   cut green beans
½ jar roasted red pepper
   strips (about 3 ounces),
   drained and slivered
⅛ teaspoon salt
⅛ teaspoon ground white
   pepper
4 ounces cream cheese
½ cup milk

¾ cup (3 ounces) blue
   cheese, crumbled
½ cup Italian-style bread
   crumbs
1 tablespoon margarine or
   butter, melted
Red and yellow bell
   pepper rose and fresh
   Italian parsley
   (optional)

PREHEAT oven to 350°F. Spray 2-quart oval casserole with nonstick cooking spray.

COMBINE green beans, red pepper strips, salt and white pepper in prepared dish.

PLACE cream cheese and milk in small saucepan; heat over low heat, stirring until melted. Add blue cheese; stir only until combined. Pour cheese mixture over green bean mixture and stir until green beans are coated.

COMBINE bread crumbs and margarine in small bowl; sprinkle evenly over casserole.

BAKE, uncovered, 20 minutes or until hot and bubbly. Garnish with bell peppers and Italian parsley, if desired. *Makes 4 servings*

Nutrients per Serving: Calories: 297, Total Fat: 20 g, Protein: 11 g, Carbohydrate: 20 g, Cholesterol: 49 mg, Sodium: 906 mg, Dietary Fiber: 1 g Dietary Exchanges: Vegetable: 2, Bread: ½, Meat: 1, Fat: 3½